THAT THING YOU DO WITH YOUR MOUTH

THAT THING YOU DO WITH YOUR MOUTH

The Sexual Autobiography of Samantha Matthews

as told to

David Shields

McSWEENEY'S
SAN FRANCISCO

McSWEENEY'S

SAN FRANCISCO

McSweeney's and colophon are registered trademarks of McSweeney's, an independent publisher with wildly fluctuating resources.

ISBN 978-1-940450-64-3

10 9 8 7 6 5 4 3 2 1

www.mcsweeneys.net

INTRODUCTION

I'VE KNOWN SAMANTHA MATTHEWS, an actress, voice-over artist, and my cousin once removed, since she was a teen-ager. (I'll be sixty next year; she just turned forty.) For a decade, I'd encouraged her to make a self-reflexive docu-mentary film about a job she occasionally moonlighted at during her first few years in Barcelona—dubbing Italian porn films into English. It seemed to me power-ful material, well worth exploring, especially since she wound up divorcing her Spanish husband. I thought per-haps the dubbing had something to do with the divorce, on a difficult-to-articulate level that she would try to articulate.

She'd gathered some footage but never was able to carve out enough time to make the film, so a couple of years ago I suggested that we work on the story together. To my horror and her own, she immediately agreed. Over eighteen months—via email, text, Skype, and FaceTime—I asked her increasingly difficult questions and she emailed back her increasingly revelatory answers (as well as several surreptitious recordings of her dubbing sessions). Initially, I thought we'd wind up with an amusing novella about America and Europe and Daisy Miller, updated to the twenty-first century. I had no idea. Samantha tunneled so deeply into her own psyche that we wound up with more than seven hundred pages, relatively few of which had anything to do with dubbing porn.

My goal was to shape all these pages into a narrative that explores what is for Samantha and for me and for many people a crucial or even *the* question: how and to what degree is it possible to get beyond early trauma?

David Shields
Seattle
January 2015

Intimacy is for strangers.
—Karen Bettencourt

I'VE BEEN TAUGHT to not apologize before any performance, and I find it annoying when actors apologize for what they're about to do, particularly during an audition, but in this case I need to do that, once; I feel terrified. If I just say it, instead of pretending to know what I'm doing, maybe I can start off on an honest path. My mind doesn't think at all linearly. I have a hard time keeping up with my thoughts and narrowing them down. I don't know. This might be a complete mess.

In no way do I want to feel like I'm being self-indulgent, talking about all of my "issues." Who gives a shit? Who am I to be telling a story? I have this intimacy-junkie part of me, though, that wants to provoke others to see something deep inside themselves. I like breaking down barriers—not to be perverse but to find a more authentic connection. Generally speaking, we're not unique.

A director once said to me, "Sam, it's so exhausting for the audience to watch you hold up all that armor. If you could stop holding it up, it would be so much easier not only for you but also for us to watch. The energy required to protect yourself just gets in the way of telling the story."

I have less and less of a need, I think, to pretend I'm a good girl. I should be professional, friendly, responsible, accommodating, easy to get along with, elegant, and graceful. Must never step out of the house without wearing at least a tiny bit of makeup, because you never know who you're going to run into. Lipstick is a winner, because my lips sort of blend in with my face. Must be confident. Don't slouch. Don't diminish yourself in public or in any conversation. Wear classic clothes, which suit you. Nothing too tight-fitting because that looks cheap. Always good to make people wonder what's under those clothes instead of shoving it in their face. Game's over, and so is their respect for you. I must foresee everyone's needs. If I'm incredibly attentive to everyone and everything around me, I can avoid all possible conflict, dangerous and trivial situations alike. No one can call me selfish, either. Don't get in the way or be irritating. Don't joke around and make silly faces with three chins (I'm really good at that) around your lover, who will then find you unattractive, even disgusting. Be aware of how big your nose is (once, on an airplane when I was fifteen, my mom told me maybe I could just get my sinuses operated on and the surgeon could do a quick little nose job while he was at it). Try to avoid the profile: not good. I should never talk about anything negative—that's a waste of energy and makes others see you as a negative person. I can smile and say yes to everything, make your life easier. Keep those nails trimmed and not painted. No, leave them a little longer, but still not painted; he doesn't like that. Don't paint your toenails; he doesn't like that, either. Be strong. No, don't. That's butchy. Seeing a difference between men and women is better. Be vulnerable, but don't cry around men, because there's a study that says the smell of women's tears actually lowers their sexual desire for you. Be mindful. Do yoga. It gives you a great ass.

Friday—how many days to Friday? It's only Tuesday. Four more days of this till I can escape.

When I was fifteen, Scott fingered me, breaking my hymen. Blood covered his hand, as though he'd punched a window. I was convinced he'd seriously disfigured me, maybe even made me sterile, for all I knew—flashes of the doctor examining my genitals at age five. After all, bad things happen to me. I'd deserve that for what I'd done. My mom was constantly reminding me of all the possible life-threatening dangers that could accompany sex and other illicit behavior. A famous basketball player died of a heart attack after trying cocaine for the first time. Basically, sex and drugs meant death. Moments before the hemorrhaging, I'd had an orgasm, dry-humping against what I now know as the biggest cock I've ever had or seen in any porn film. I didn't tell him I came. After cleaning up all the mess, I walked him out to say goodbye, and as I hugged him good night, I fainted. An orgasm and a wrecked vagina were all a little too much.

I lost my virginity to Scott at his best friend's house while the friend's parents were away for the weekend. I lied and said I was staying at Dawn's. She covered for me. It was planned a week in advance. The guest room was all set up. It was a granny's room: perfect and sterile with a *Little House on the Prairie* flower-print comforter on a queen-size bed I'm positive we must have stained in a way that made it look like a nasty murder had taken place. I was giving birth the other way around, and he came into a condom. Proud of myself and crippled, I showered, water stinging me horrifically.

I'm aroused by distance/coldness.

I want someone to know what they want and not fumble around trying to please me. I want them to go for it; I like the roughness sometimes. I've always liked that dark, perverse stare, the dangerous, mysterious-looking guy, almost mean-looking, the 9½ *Weeks* Mickey Rourke. Even the way he treats her badly makes her want him more—that's sexy to me, just like Carl, my oldest half brother, handsome and mysterious and scary. At nineteen I found myself wanting him to desire me. Did I invite him to treat me the way he did that Thanksgiving more than twenty years ago? I feel shameful for desiring something I know is twisted.

An open, serious stare from afar that continues during sex… looking straight into your soul with their desire… knowing you desire them just as much. That's possible only with chemistry. I can't fake that. I'm sure my ex-husband, Jaume, would have liked me to look at him that way. You simply can't force desire. Maybe you can fake it in porn, but I doubt it. In the dozens of porn films I've dubbed from Italian into English, I think I've seen one couple that had that chemistry.

Maybe by watching these uninhibited women for so many years, I've come to see it as normal—why couldn't you be "base" with someone if there was mutual attraction? I envy the women's openness. They're dangerous in the way they fuck. I want to be like that. To say, *Yes, I like that*, and *Do that to me*, and to be completely open with my body, wanton—I'm reclaiming what I wasn't allowed to want and feel, which of course only heightens the desire.

In many ways, I'm not masochistic or self-destructive at all. I'm assertive about my career, etc., but there are things in my makeup that stifle and baffle me.

Michael and I were on the high school varsity swim team together in Scottsdale. He was on steroids. It was the '90s and it was cool to be buff. He told me my legs were huge, I had a big nose and horse teeth, but he was used to all these things. Awww shucks, thanks. I was blessed that he could let go of all these disfigurements and still love me. Which I still believe today. He did only point out the obvious; it just wasn't nice. One night, our tickling fight turned into pinching and biting, which he did so hard that on prom night I had to put makeup all over my arms to hide it, the dress covering the wounds on my legs. Despite my starvation and makeup, you can still see the evidence in the prom photos, which should be titled *Bruised Barbie*.

Pre-prom night, we went to the tanning salon and had a competition over who could be more chocolate; that hurt, too. He won. He always won—until one night, when I suddenly stopped caring and hated him instantly. I kicked him so hard on the side of his thigh that I whipped both of his feet out from underneath him. Me, my 110 pounds to his 180. To this day, I have no idea how I was physically capable of it.

Some people don't like sex, some people like sex but don't see it as an especially important part of their life, and some people see sex as a journey. It's never been a minor part of my life, even when I wasn't having sex regularly for years.

I've stopped hoping I can fuck William tonight. Two days ago was plenty for the next couple weeks, right? Barricades are up. Man space. Leave me alone. He keeps me at arm's length, keeps the feral girl down. He's rationing. I'm in the sex breadline.

The further into man space he goes, the more I desire him. *Cuando te prohibe algo, despierta el deseo.* His what-I-feel-as-a-lack-of-desire for me makes me want to drown myself in a bottle of wine, smoke a pack of cigarettes, find a corner with a curtain where my libido can be naked, and do a jig. Definitely not a jig—that has to be the least sexy dance in the world. A pole dance would be better (which I secretly would love to try, but no one wants to see me pole dance now that I'm forty...). Aaaaand this is when I need to scream. I'm a petulant child. "You should talk to David about that," he says. "Foot-stamping. You love a good foot-stamp, dontcha, darling?"

I got him to turn off the TV after six hours of sports today. I think that's enough. I don't think I'm being unreasonable. I'm sitting in his place on the sofa. I don't know how that happened, that this is his space on the sofa. I'm a sofa-spot enabler. I'm irritated now and want him out of the back of the house. He looks shocked and amused. As if the shit on the TV were close to silent, as if what was on there were gentle and fun. Hands in the air, like, *Oh so sorry, your majesty.* I'm just annoyed 'cause I want to fuck him. What's wrong with me? Had he rolled me in the hay, he could have watched the tennis match, the darts match, footie, cricket, and Formula 1 at deafening volume all day long.

I think I've been horny all my life and finally I have someone I'm horny for. He says I should take up painting again. Why can't I be horny for painting?

Now that I finally have a partner I'm extremely attracted to, it feels almost like an addiction. I always want more. I'm never satisfied. I don't understand why he doesn't want it all the time. That's never happened to me before. If he were all over me, surely I wouldn't want it, as he's told me himself. Do you think in any couple both people desire each other equally? I'm constantly staring at him. When he comes into the room after showering, I'm waiting for him to drop his towel so I can get a peek at him. I find him so incredibly sexy. But just him. No one else. In a joking way, he says I love him for his cock, but he's not joking. His cock *is* him; it's imbued by his person.

In a tantrum the other day, I said to him maybe we should just be buddies, since that's pretty much all we are, anyway. Maybe we can sip hot chocolate together and play Sudoku. Let's make a date, go out to dinner, not talk, and read our own newspapers. Let's be settled. Let's be normal. Bland. Beige. Let's die. Together.

I have man legs; William has lady legs. I hate it when both of us are wearing shorts and you can see our shadows on the pavement. I'm nearly a foot shorter than he is and my leg shadows are bigger. I always hope he isn't noticing that.

Were William's exes sexy? I find myself feeling it's somehow unfair I haven't screwed these girls as well. Do they have porn pussies, all perfect and neat and little, or the lettuce leaf hanging between the two lips? I used to get one of my exes to tell me what his other girlfriends' pussies looked like. I don't know if it made me feel better or worse. I think better. Yeah.

After we'd been together six months, William told me, "I still fancy you, but it's not like I want to jump you all the time." Thanks. Why didn't you just say while yawning, "I can still see you, but just barely"?

I have such a positive attitude in relationships: he always tells me I can't help finding the tragedy. If there's nothing wrong, which according to him there rarely is (unless I'm drinking), I'll find something wrong. I don't disagree. I need to foresee the possible disasters, be prepared for the worst so I won't be shocked when *it* happens, whatever *it* is.

(*After the man turns on the stereo, they make love on the bed—the man on top of the woman, who's fighting images of the porn she filmed yesterday: "Fuck me!" "Oooooohhh yeah." "Lick my pussy." "Hello, I'm the preacher's wife." "You like that, don't you?" Different actors say each line. Trying to concentrate on her partner, she's swept up in the porno images. After sex, they lie together in bed.*)
   How was it for you?
   Good. You?
   Good. I thought it was going to be more intense and then suddenly it wasn't. But good, good.
   (*Pause.*)
   Yeah, me, too.
   (*Pause.*)
   I felt like maybe you were thinking a little.
   Yeah, I was. I was really in my head today.
   Yeah, I thought so.
   (*Pause.*)

Why?

I don't know.

What were you thinking about?

Nothing in particular—just, I don't know, maybe I was taking too long…

But you were like that from the beginning. I felt it right when we hit the bed.

I don't know. I guess I was just thinking about pleasing you too much.

You know you can't do that.

I know.

In answer to your question, I would say Yes, being the object of someone's desire feels dominant to me. The other person surrenders in their desire, and there's a softness and vulnerability when their desire is expressed. That gives me room to get in there and take over. It's like they're under a spell; they lose control. As long as they desire me, I can do what I want. If the other person has no desire for me, or if the desire isn't as strong, I lose my power, not just my sexual power. The two are intertwined. I'm sure subliminally I was taught that the other person was more malleable if they were weakened by desire.

I thrive on turning someone on, being the object of their desire. I once had a butch-femme relationship with Traci, a cop who looked like k.d. lang and who barely touched me. I was interested only in pleasing her, having that power. Having always been the dominant one, she flipped out (in a good way) over how opposite her role was with me. With people I'm in love with, I'm much more flexible.

Thanks for the copy of *A Mother in History*. I look forward to, even crave, the shockers—not for their content or Stafford's intent to shock, but for their element of surprise, that knife edge of intimacy.

I think my obsession with communication, desire for real intimacy, is directly related to never knowing from one moment to the next if my mom was going to be Carol or Kitty. Carol was the repressed post-1950s mother, scaring me out of having sex, leaving me newspaper clippings in my bathroom drawer about prim-and-proper young ladies dying from AIDS upon losing their virginity. Carol was the one who told me, "When you sleep with someone, you're giving yourself away," and "Once they've had sex with you, there's no challenge anymore and they lose interest." And

Kitty I would find passed out, face down on my bed when I came home with my boyfriend. Kitty would tell me every tragedy that had ever happened to her and talk about how sexy she really was, how she and my dad used to have sex constantly. Is that where I get all this from?

People I'm drawn to are strong, a bit masculine, a little mentally unstable (I can be the nurturer), self-confident, funny, and *aggressive*...

I've started seeing a new therapist, and that's been consuming me. With her I talk about my feelings as if they belonged to someone else—could be my handy ol' disassociation tool. Lately, I feel both connected and disconnected. Does that make sense?

Does that happen to you when you're writing about "naked" things? Do you ever feel vulnerable or worried how it may come across when you write your "secrets"?

I can hardly go more than a day or two without seeing some part of Gaudi's Sagrada Família out of the corner of my eye. Counting the ways I hate that thing...

I always sensed my dad had a secret life. He's eternally curious and passionate about the most minute details in life, sees beauty everywhere. I'd cuddle up in his lap and we'd play duets of "Heart and Soul" together, his strong, square, padded-cushion fingers interlaced with mine. "Hold on," he'd say when we were listening to a song we loved, "it's coming, right now right now… and… here! Listen to this!" I sang in a high-pitched voice to the Bee Gees, laughing hysterically, and he'd tell me I had a great ear. Searching for gnomes in the fantasia forest in our backyard; staring at the formidable beauty of the Olympic Mountains in the skyline—there was magic and feeling in everything, something huge and heartfelt. He was moved and moved me. He has also acted on beauty everywhere.

I remember finding a *Playboy* in his bottom dresser drawer when I was fifteen, and that was the first confirmation of what I'd suspected. Not that *Playboy* represents anything, really. I just knew in my gut he'd had affairs, which were later confirmed when I was around nineteen. To be honest, that part doesn't really bother me at all. As I get older, I find myself following in some of his footsteps, or the ones I recognize—trying to find the adventure, the gems hidden under the rocks, and knowing I can't share that with everyone.

The first month William and I were together, I was explosively in love with him; I remember saying I was always looking for the celebration in life. I'd just come out of my marriage to Jaume. I didn't want boring, settled. I wanted a connection and I wanted to feel it as often as I could, since any day could be my last. I'm sure I sounded manic. I was showing him how excited I was to be with him and how much I loved him, how ready I was for an adventure together, and hoping to find an ease in that, a joy—again, just like my dad had taught me. William fell silent and shut down. My enthusiasm for life has always inspired others and led them to a tidal high; now it was as though I'd told him I'd had a sex change or something.

He said what I'd said had scared him: he wasn't capable of being exciting all the time and normal/settled is a good thing. To him, I represented instability rather than freedom. My whole body sank into the chair and something clicked in me. I knew from then on I wouldn't be able to share this ecstatic side I had. He'd never feel it that way; he'd just feel scared of it. In my love I'm not unpredictable, but in the way I live life, I like to be spontaneous, and if there's trust, shouldn't anything be possible? (Don't answer.)

I almost never talk passionately with William about anything in my life, really. And when I do, I have to make sure I say it only once, because if I repeat it for the sake of weight, it immediately loses its value for him. It's also an American/British thing. We—Americans—are known for being overemphatic, exaggerated. That, mixed with me being what he calls a "thesp," is something he doesn't fully understand, so now I let out my passionate side with my girlfriends, my friends, and with him I curb it. A friend said to me at the very beginning of my relationship with William, "You're too big for him. He's not going to be able to handle you." Whatever that means. I don't think I'm too big. I just think we experience life very differently.

So what I'm trying to say is I feel a lot like my dad—living a separate, passionate life outside of my relationship. I don't want to be with anyone other than William; it's not even my choice. It's just the way it is. I'm passionately in love with him. Is there such a thing as being passionately in love and sharing all your passions with the same person? I haven't found it. Doesn't mean I have to, either, I guess.

My mother is threatened by the world. She's trapped in her past (I am, too, obviously), an eternal victim, and she lives her life believing she deserved better—which someone should have given to her. The spiritual wisdom she studies is just an excuse to look away from herself, to bask in cliché poetry, to dream we're all one, we're energy; I can even get into that, just not with her. For her it's something separate, an escape, and for me all that energy is just a link to deeper honesty (or so I tell myself). She floats around in her head, ruminating about a more elevated life, a gentleness, a kindness, sending me quotes from self-help authors and ancient healers. Her favorite word is *grace*, which bugs the hell out of me.

When she's on her pain meds, her eyes are gray and cloudy; there's a wall behind them, a world going on in there that only she knows. (There's an openness, a clarity and sadness, in my dad's eyes. When I see him standing alone, playing with the change in his pocket, he seems lonely. He looks sad, and I feel sorry for him… I know I'm completely incapable of holding my father accountable for not protecting my mother and me. I needed him to represent some sort of tangible lifeline outside of the freak show/snuff movie that was happening at home. I liked that he traveled to Japan on long business trips, and often; that way, I could see that it was in fact possible to escape, even if just temporarily. Which gave me some sort of hope; ridiculously, it still does.)

My mom is never willing to let you know fully what she thinks, unless she's drunk and then you really don't want to know those thoughts, because the next day she'll pretend they were never spoken and you'll lose your mind trying to talk honestly about those "nonexistent things." Her thoughts go round and round and get all mixed up, contradicting themselves.

Christmas and Easter and Thanksgiving, she wants to sit around a perfect table set with the family china, crystal, and sterling silver cutlery, and have everyone sing Christmas carols and look at her adoringly, even though she's actually been "napping" all day. She's "civilized" and dreaming rather than experiencing. She lives an idea of how life should be, not how it actually is. I'm constantly throwing reality in her face and she can't bear it (not to say, of course, that I don't cling to my own set of illusions).

She was raised to get married and be taken care of, as most women of her generation were, and she remained loyal to that idea/ideal, so she resents my father for not having delivered on it. She's angry and ashamed and very, very hurt. I know she loves me, but she loves me as her teddy bear. She loves me needily. She probably thought I'd be the one who would love her always. I do. And I will. But now with distance. Her dishonesty has pushed me away. I'm tired of pretending she's fine. The sad thing is, underneath all of that there's a very loving, intelligent, funny woman. Wickedly funny. A drop of liquor and her quick wit and lashing tongue fire out at my dad, making everyone laugh at his expense. She's just lost and trying to pretend she's not. I'm lost and trying to admit I am.

As University of Washington undergraduates, Jake and I were the love interests in a play about the suffrage movement at the beginning of the twentieth century. He had a straight, sandy-blond ponytail that went down to the middle of his back—didn't really work for the time period we were depicting, but oh well. He put it in a low bun. I remember thinking that wasn't very sexy. He wasn't the best actor, but he'd known and survived "real life." I was twenty and couldn't imagine how I was going to be able to support myself with a real job. He was twenty-six, had gravity, was gentle, raced bicycles (and as a result, had very muscular, shaved legs). I'd started messing around with girls before dating him. He made out with one of my best gay male friends at a gay club—a big, open-mouthed, face-engulfing kiss—to show he was open to homosexuality. That was bad acting and it bugged me.

He had that serious, intense look Carl had and pouty, square lips, which reminded me of my great grandpa (a little weird). Similar square hands, movements. I could imagine his lips turning into the lips my great grandfather had at ninety, from a pout to a sag—a little bit of drool on the sides. That grossed me out, too.

He didn't tell me he had a girlfriend. He invited me over one Saturday morning to his studio apartment to "rehearse" outside of rehearsals. We rehearsed how we were going to have sex later. We would have sex after he told his girlfriend he didn't want to be with her anymore. She was in the audience directly across from us the same evening, and she wasn't very happy to see her boyfriend with a date later that night. I thought the whole thing was a little sketchy: he had to try me out first, then he could leave her. Still, I understood.

We started dating, and I started seeing a psychologist. I'd come back from my weekly therapy sessions and Jake would ask me how they went and then we would talk about everything I'd said and he'd analyze everything I'd just analyzed. He started to get inside my brain, question every sigh, every smile, every movement. I let him. I became his patient. I needed all the help I could get but couldn't handle the brain invasion. I had no space for myself anymore. He was always either sleeping with me, eating with me, or looking at me very closely. Another thing he did that bugged me: when he made tuna sandwiches, he slowly and meticulously scraped every last teeny-tiny bit of tuna out of the tin can.

He was the manager for a building of tiny studio apartments with Murphy beds. On Capitol Hill—slightly dumpy verging on ghetto. He hired me as his assistant for ten bucks an hour to help renovate apartments when the weirdos moved out. (One tenant went to jail and had a collection of girls' driver's licenses in his greasy kitchen drawer. He worked in the morgue, would go and collect the dead bodies from crime scenes, and kept a collection of the girls' ID cards. Shiver. We had to cut his sofa in half with a chain saw to get it out of the apartment.) I had my first doggy-style orgasm with Jake on the floor of one of those nasty places.

He was an avid hiker-camper-outdoorsman. We went camping in areas where there were bears. He knew how to do all that stuff and made me feel safe about it.

One day I asked him how many girls he'd slept with and he said approximately five hundred. What?! He said the best way to get to know someone is to sleep with them. The more quickly the better. Direct entry past their persona. In my head, my mom called him a sleaze-ball sex addict. How could he just sleep with anyone?

Did he have no criteria? Did he care only about fucking? I was so mad. Surely he was going to fuck somebody else while fucking me. He clearly couldn't control himself. I wanted him to want only me, even though I didn't even really want him that much in the first place. I had no power over him. I wanted to possess him. Or did I? What was I to him? A body? How could he possibly be attracted to that many people? *That was sick*, I thought to myself. *That was wrong. He had a problem. I wasn't allowed to do what he did.* I was fucking jealous!

He told me he'd fucked this red-headed Goth lighting designer (who looked to me like a horse—she probably was reasonably attractive, but I was mad and wanted to see her that way) while he was with the girlfriend he left for me. When I broke up with him, I called his ex and we met for coffee. I apologized to her for running off with him, then told her he'd fucked the red-headed Goth girl behind her back. The two girls were friends. Boy, did I fuck him up for all of his promiscuity. My mom was on my side. He shall not sin. Especially if I can't.

Years after we broke up, he was attacked by a grizzly bear when he got between the mother and her cubs. He survived by hiking five miles to safety with a crushed skull. A couple of years ago I heard he fell from a cliff while camping alone and died.

RRRRRRAARR!

Oh yeah, baby, I love it when you growl. You tiger! You animal!

RRRRRRRAAAAAAARRRR!

Oh, yeah, one more time. Come on—it turns me on.

(Louder) RRRRAAAARR!

(In ecstasy) YYYYYeah! Whew!

You like that, huh?

Fuck yeah!

In grad school I went through a "lesbian phase," as my mother puts it. The Christmas I got engaged to Jaume, my parents came to visit me in Barcelona; we went out for dinner and I decided to tell them about my ex-girlfriends. I wanted to explain to them how positive these experiences had been, how they'd given me my power back. Surely it would be nice for them to know I didn't see all sexual relationships as negative: I was "healthy" and not as damaged as I'd thought I was by my past. After all, my mom had told me to always be open with her about how I was dealing with everything, including especially the abuse.

With women, I felt adored and open, unafraid. It was virgin territory—innocent, clean. I felt a strength and a femininity emerging from me that I'd always hidden.

I didn't need to protect myself from them. In general, girlfriends (I'm talking about nonsexual relationships) always tell you the things guys don't—what they specifically like about your body, your mind; they listen to you and are sincerely interested (or they're really good at faking it). That, combined with a lover, was exceptional, almost otherworldly.

I didn't go into much detail that night with my family. My dad just said he wanted me to be happy, and if that's what it was, well, then so be it. My mother completely shut down, saying that was something she was very uncomfortable with. She didn't like it, didn't agree with it, and simply couldn't share in my happiness about it. I saw that look of panic in her eyes: the devil was inside her daughter. Her look was, *Oh god, she's been brainwashed.* We fought about it for years—my frustration with her not being able to accept it, her rigidity with the subject. I think deep down inside there's a part of her that's like me, and that scares the shit out of her.

Starting with my first boyfriend, when I was thirteen, at least five of my boyfriends have been not-nice. Another at fifteen, Scott, then Cameron, and I would say even William falls into that category. He and I have a vulnerability together I didn't have with the other four, but we're very volatile. He can be quite cutting, dismissive. My first boyfriend dumped me and I remember thinking, *I'm never gonna let that happen again.*

Cameron was tall, pale, and very slight, gangly; I could never make out the shape of his body under his baggy clothes—I spent many days trying to imagine it. He was always hunched over, sitting in a chair and spinning his hair around his index and middle fingers, intensely looking at you as though you were a lab experiment. A very intellectual college student who was trying to be an actor but completely blocked by his demons. His sexuality was nonexistent, and he was little-boyishly pretty. This unidentifiable sexuality was fascinating to me. I couldn't imagine him having sex at all. Grrrrrrr.

He cast me in a play he wrote, and I made him laugh really hard. I was a clown and saw I could crack him a little. One night at a party I'd had a few drinks, was happily confident, and told a friend I thought Cameron (who was there that night) was sexy. She warned me off, telling me to be careful because he was known for being a total womanizer, slept with everyone—her two best friends and both of them at the same time. She thought he might break my heart; I was insulted. How about him being worried I might break his? This became a game, a dare. I was going to be the next one, make him fall in love with me, then dump him.

His then-girlfriend left the party and he and I made out on the front lawn. Two weeks later, he left his girlfriend and had practically moved in to my apartment. At first he was amazingly open and direct, loving, even worried he might not be able to get an erection, because that's always what happened to him at the beginning of relationships, when he was falling in love. His respect for the other, his vulnerability (according to his mom!) made it difficult for him to get it up at first. That happened once and never again. Actually, it never happened. He just worried it would. He went from falling in love to in lust and then one night I awoke to his hand on my face holding me down and within two seconds he was fucking me, or someone in his dreams.

We used every sex toy ever made. He tied me up, shaved himself and me, handcuffed me, threw me around, upside down, had me in positions I didn't know were even possible. We didn't make love. It was always dirty. He fucked me, sometimes looking me in the eyes, or on other days putting a pillow over my head a couple minutes before he came. That was borderline weird/

scary. (Oooh, did I actually feel a boundary there?) He was dangerous and perverse. Maybe it opened up that little-girl-doing-something-naughty side of me. I liked it and hated it, started to learn I could get pleasure out of it and not feel guilty about it, either, but there was no real connection between us other than when we had sex. He let a vulnerable fox out in our sexland, then hid in his *New Republic* articles the rest of the time. I wanted the part of him that came out during sex to be there when we weren't having sex—the beginning of my intimacy-junkieness. He told me to leave him alone. That's how he was and he wasn't going to share that side of himself anywhere else.

His constant need to have sex became an unbearable lashing. I felt like a dead horse. Two months went by without us having sex, according to him, and he began angrily jerking off to porno magazines while lying next to me. It disgusted me. But before it disgusted me it thrilled me.

Two years into the relationship, on a cross-country road trip, I found myself bent over naked in a divey hotel room with a paper bag over my head, my hands bound together, and him photographing me with our Polaroid camera. A memory of me. Of someone. A body. I threw all the photos away. My mom didn't even have to say anything; I knew I'd done something really fucked up—letting him photograph me like a whore. Who knew where those pictures could have ended up?

A year later I dumped him over the phone. He threw the phone across the room in a rage, screaming, "No one will ever love you the way I love you!"

He was right.

I've been watching you all night and I think you're incredible.

Thank you.

I'm a painter and I'd like to paint your portrait.

Oh really?

Yes. Come to my room: 507.

Oh I don't know.

I'll pay you.

Uh—

You're so gorgeous I have to have you on canvas.

Well, okay.

God, you're beautiful. Can you just spread your legs a little more?

Like this? Mmhh.

That's it. Yeaaah. I've got to get to know my subjects more personally, you know, before I can paint them.

Oh yeah?
Why don't you take off that pretty little dress of yours?
Okay. Is that better?

My movement teacher in the acting program at Ohio State would lead us through physical exercises that sometimes would evoke unpleasant sensations. He challenged us to look at the new sensations as simply different—things we'd never felt before. "Different" didn't have to be scary. With repetition, the different sensations became part of our sensory vocabulary.

After a month doing a one-woman show off-off-Broadway, I returned to my grad program and a big night out with my classmates at a club. I was feeling high, free, excited to be alive, hopeful, and very happy to have been paid (very little) to do theater in New York—my future acting career ahead of me. On the dance floor with my classmates, all of whom I'd been in boot camp with for the past year and a half, I felt safe and powerful. I turned my head and saw this beautiful smile on a gorgeous, playful face. She had sexy eyes. I swear there was a spotlight on her.

I edged closer to her and thought she must be a professional break-dancer. I was in a long-distance relationship that was already over in my head—just hadn't gotten around to making the phone call yet. I wanted her (the break-dancer) immediately. I smelled her. I felt her already. She was a very pretty little boy. We exchanged names, smiles, lusty glances, and some dancing nice and close, but no touching. Without even thinking, I said, "Wanna come home with me?" "I think I'd rather take you to dinner," Kelly answered back with the formality of a gentleman from the 1950s. I think I laughed. It was hard to take this little guy seriously, saying something like that. She was shorter than me but very confident. She had a little bit of a ghetto vibe going on, too (weird combo, I know—ghetto gentleman), that to me was completely unfamiliar and rough. It was weirdly sexy.

Since I wasn't able to get her to come back home with me, I had to make her see she'd made a mistake. Let her stew on it for a while, wondering if she'd missed her chance. I didn't call her for a couple weeks. I finally called and we met for a coffee that turned into hard alcohol and smoking cigarettes back at her flat. She told me she vacuumed every day, maybe twice. Things were in control there. (When she was little, her mom used to drag her out of bed by the hair at 5 a.m. and make her scrub the walls. One morning, most of her hair stayed on the pillow.)

I don't think we kissed until she walked me back to my flat. We started to make out on my sofa and I went in for the kill. I remember her stopping my hands at every advance. Why? Again, she said she'd rather take it slow. She left me like a sixteen-year-old boy with blue balls.

The next time, we fucked on her living room floor to really loud, deep tech house. It was passionate and she was so open with her body. That impressed me. I wanted to be like her one day. I think right after, or worse, maybe even before, she told me she was still obsessed with her last girlfriend, Melanie. She still had a picture of her up in her room, covering the private bits but giving you very important information. Melanie was petite, blonde, and had huge tits—a sort of young Marilyn Monroe sex appeal, the total opposite of me. I was inadequate and now liked Kelly even more. She was unconquerable and fucking great in bed/on the floor.

She said we should just keep it simple: be friends who would sleep together. Okay! I wanted her to be my serious girlfriend but pretended I didn't. That went on for six months.

Kelly broke a supposed coke habit by joining the military. She went to boot camp, where she pretended to be straight, came back tougher and drug-free, and many days was really nasty to me. Six months in, she'd randomly show up after not talking to me for maybe a week, drunk (but still sharp) and sweet, and seduce me. Then we wouldn't talk for a few days. One day she told me she just wanted to be friends. She still loved Melanie. I cried (after Kelly left). She broke my heart, but I told her that was better for me, too. We managed to stay friends-with-benefits over the next eight months or so, sleeping together whenever we weren't dating other people. The rescue fuck.

One day she picked me up in her car and drove around, ripping into me—saying the cruelest things. There were several sessions like this where she would shout me down or laugh at me, tell me to go fuck myself, and leave me crying on the corner. I hadn't done anything but be there when she needed me for a laugh or a hug or a screw. She wanted only to hurt me, the one person who was a constant for her.

I remember kissing her and looking at her the way I looked at my boyfriends and thinking that was so weird and cool and natural and exciting. I loved her and she was a woman. That was the first time I'd ever looked at a woman that way. I began to see boys walking down the street as little lesbians everywhere. I cut off all my practically waist-length hair for a production of *The Taming of the Shrew*. I think she was a little less in love with me after that.

She liked me to almost fist her but would never let herself orgasm with me. She couldn't go there. She had to dominate me or I had to be rough with her. That was so hot, these unspoken sex rules of hers. She was serious about it. I prefer serious. By just looking at me—her mouth slightly open, gauging me, leading me, pushing me, telling me how it was going to be through her stare—she could practically make me come. She decided she loved me and imagined us getting married. Too late. I was in love with someone else.

I'm definitely sexually attracted to a darkness. I want to win over the other. I do that even with William today.

Sitting downstairs in a café below our house, I'm feeling angry for no particular reason. Don't you love my constant mood swings? Sometimes I think I must be mildly manic-depressive...

I used to hate/love when this guy I was with would say, "You can't get enough of that, can you?"

Okay, you guys, I know it's your first day, but I can't hear you. You've got to make some noise, or these scenes are really boring to watch. And use some variation. Break it up with some "Oh yeah baby," "Fuck me harder," "Suck my dick," "Lick my pussy." You know. And she can come more than once. You can't just all the time be doing "Oh! Oh! Oh! Oh!" You've got to break it up with "Oh, I'm gonna come! OH!"

Good question: Do I think of myself as hyper-sexualized?
    Do other people?
    Do you?

When I have a sexual desire for someone and it's not returned, I think I must be disgusting. My hidden grossness must somehow have escaped. I've been discovered.

I have only a few concrete memories of the abuse, which happened from when I was two to when I was five. There was no penetration, to my memory, and according to the doctor, there hadn't been, but everything else that could be done was done. I have images/feelings, marking the ages, from two different houses we lived in, in West Bloomfield (Detroit suburb). The boys were from Dad's previous marriage. Carl and Jesse were twelve and thirteen years older than me.

Carl was always around the corner or about to come home or pop out from who knows where, but always waiting to freak the shit out of me, lock me in a closet, hang me by my feet over the railing from the third landing of the staircase, or put a plastic bag over my head—like a killer whale with a sea lion, playing with it, torturing it, loving it, laughing at my fear.

To this day I can't watch *Star Trek* because I remember it playing in Jesse's bedroom when he'd do his thing with me; I remember him identifying a pair of underwear as being sexy (they were orange and black and satiny and felt kind of adult-like), taking them off me, and licking me down there like a dog would lick a wound, asking me if I liked it. I felt tense and weird, as if I were supposed to like it, and I told him I did, to make him feel okay about it. I remember going numb when he did that to me and staring at the blue light glowing on the ceiling, focusing in on that and disappearing until he'd stop.

I felt sorry for him. He told me this was "our secret" and I should never tell anyone about it. There was a horrible, musky stench, of unwashed sheets and a fat, sweaty body. He wanted me to touch him and I remember thinking it was disgusting. It was sticky and smelly. I hated that part the most. Penises were the most disgusting things ever. His was. Jesse abused me while supposedly babysitting me. I asked my mom why white stuff came out of his penis.

Carol would drink herself into Kitty, shaking in terror of my half brothers and holding me as her teddy bear to calm herself down. She was pregnant and had begun teaching me how babies were made. She soon lost the baby after Carl beat her up one night in front of me. I stayed with friends for a few days while she was in the hospital.

I had a little blond five-year-old boyfriend I got caught with under the bed, naked. I told him how to make babies and he wanted to try, but I told him no because I might get pregnant. Upon being discovered, I was scolded and he wasn't allowed to come over again. It was my fault and I was a bad, dirty person. His parents now thought I was, too.

Yes, a girl can reach orgasm by age five, which is when I discovered I could masturbate. One day, when I started rubbing up against the dinner table, I was told very abruptly not to. The response from my mom felt shocking; I'd done something wrong and was never to do it again. "That's something you do in private"—which could have been okay, but her tone was so harsh.

I did it constantly, in my own room; I was the only one who could make myself feel bad about it, which I always did. I thought my genitals looked different from everyone else's, and I was always covering up. I also remember always wearing underwear in front of my dad because I was a girl and he was a boy and that part of me was not to be shown to him. I thought he might do something to me, too, if he saw me "down there." Whenever I went into my parents' bed in the middle of the night for a cuddle and they stroked my back to calm me, I always had the (quite irrational) fear their hands might wander to the wrong place. My body was everyone else's except mine.

My mom would say, "It's really important for you to be able to talk about it. You've been sexually abused, Sam. I want you to know you can talk about it whenever you want." So I did: at age eight, I told all my friends I'd been sexually abused by my brother "when I was a child," because this was supposed to make me feel better—talking about it. I knew how to talk about what happened but felt nothing; they did. I'd observe people's expressions when I told the story. It was as if it had happened to someone else.

Interesting that you should choose to ask me now how I view my own physical appearance, as that very same theme came up over the last few days and led to an explosion of tears the other night. I was cast in what will supposedly become a TV series. The guy who is producing it, directing it, and starring in it is an American actor I worked with last year on a film. The premise and script of the series are really sharp, and I was flattered that he cast me, felt/feel a pressure to do well, etc. He was going to introduce my character later on, but at the last minute he decided to put me in the teaser. I knew nothing about my character, and when I went for my makeup test, the costume designer said the only thing she knew was I was supposed to be very sexy—the first time anyone has cast me in a role like this.

I received the script for the teaser two days before shooting, and my lines didn't give me any more information about who I was. On the day of the shoot, I thought surely the director would let me know more about the role, but he was very busy running around, so I didn't dare ask him. Finally, I asked him in a sort of jokey way, "So, Thomas, ya know, any information about what I'm doing here?" He said, "Well, basically, let's just say you're the sex kitten of the show. Do all your lines with that in mind. Everything should have an erotic undertone to it." Gulp.

I was supposed to say the first line staring directly into the camera, which for me is always the most difficult thing to do. I like to work off of people and forget about myself. I saw my reflection and didn't like the makeup job—bags under my eyes and a giant mosquito bite above my left eyebrow, which I immediately asked the makeup artist to cover up. She'd done what most makeup artists do: the minimal thing, making my tiny eyes disappear into my face. Eyes are everything; if the audience can't see them, you have no power, and I felt ugly. I could tell the DP was having difficulty lighting my face to get that sex-kitten look and I had to feel confident regardless.

To me, a sex kitten is a model, an Angelina Jolie. I felt short and squatty, my quads massive. One absurd Thanksgiving when I was nineteen, Jesse and Carl were invited to our house on Vashon Island. I hadn't seen them or talked to them since I was about eleven. My dad thought it was a good idea to get the darling boys back in the house after an eight-year absence, for a family reunion. I thought it was especially wonderful to catch up with them since Jesse had just made his TV debut on *Oprah Winfrey*, claiming to be a recovered rapist. He took me aside and apologized for abusing me, then he and my parents went to bed, leaving me up with Carl, who'd brought along his chef's knife collection, as you do. He began to study my body with that look I was supposed to give the camera, telling me the reason brothers are always jealous of their sisters' boyfriends is because they really just want to fuck their sisters. And he wanted to smell me and lick me and make me come. After all, I owed it to him, as my dad had abandoned him and he'd been living on the streets for years. I was sitting in a chair and he knelt down in front of me, grabbing my calves, massaging them and saying, "Ahhh. Too bad you got the Matthews legs." *The big, ugly, unfeminine legs* is what he was saying: *You're lucky I even find you attractive.* This is what I'm fighting in my head, trying to push away, as the camera rolls and the director calls, "Action!" Carl's look is nasty, wrong, and I'm supposed to give the exact same look now, but I feel everyone can read what's going through my head. I'm exposed—vulnerable, scared. I feel my face trembling.

I managed to battle my way through the first close-ups and the director said, "We got it. I know it feels really mechanical, but you'll see: it's just going to be quick flashes, and with editing it'll work just fine." The whole thing has become a farce. They took a risk by giving me this role, and now they can see I'm definitely not a sex kitten. They're definitely going to cut me out of the series. (I'm waiting for an email from the director saying he's going to go with someone else. And out of embarrassment, I don't dare "like" any of the Facebook photos of the shoot.)

On my way home I stopped by our local restaurant and found my friend, the owner, sitting outside. I was hoping he'd be there, because I needed a drink. I needed not to feel humiliated. Focusing on the job and talking about it positively and numbing out all the detestable feelings would be the answer. I ended up meeting a couple girlfriends later, didn't eat any dinner, and got quite hammered. I was now celebrating the idea of being cast and cracking jokes about the shoot.

I get home and William and I start watching an episode of *The Killing* in bed. There's a scene in which the female cop discovers the councilman's emails that are evidence he's the rapist-murderer of a young girl. The computer screen lighting the dark, empty room where the cop is looking at the emails; and then suddenly the murderer behind her, his terrifying silhouette, asking her what she's doing—all this takes me back to watching *Star Trek* with Jesse in that dark, blue-lit room. The fear, locked in there, no escape. And on the other side of that bedroom, the other brother waiting to hunt me. I lost it and broke into sobs, pressing my face into my pillow, and told William to turn it off. A feeling of disgust came over me. This fucked-up, ugly, Matthews-legged girl, spiraling into a pile of shit, mulling around in it, going darker and darker, thinking there's no way anyone would be capable of finding me attractive, and even if I were beautiful, my mental state would be such a massive turnoff.

My eyes have been swollen for two days now—yet another physical manifestation of the mess inside me. I can't hide it. I just want to stay home and be left alone until it passes, but I can't because I've got to take Roc and Ava to their after-school activities and talk to mothers with whom I have nothing in common, pretending all is fine.

So, basically there are two ways to give a blow job: you can either do it like this, with your hand—mmm mmm—or some people do it like this—mm mm mm. You'll find what you like better. You can do the same thing for kissing and the other effects.

I met Jaume in Columbus at our graduate acting program's beginning-of-the-year picnic. He wore his pants above his waist with a tight little belt and had fluffy, wavy hair and sweet, gentle, sparkly eyes. He was warm and foreign (Spanish) and verging on geeky. Not at all my type. We lived in adjacent buildings for six months or so and caught the same bus every morning at the same time. I used to avoid speaking to him, because he was annoyingly chipper. Always a smile on his face; everything was wonderful and jolly. I was in a mood most mornings, from having stayed up scandalously late the night before, drinking and smoking and dancing at the lesbian bars and stumbling home two hours before 8 a.m. class. Now it was 7:50 Tuesday morning. I was a fuckup and he was a perfect little puppy, not gauging that anyone else might not feel like talking.

We were cast opposite each other as the love interests in one of the last plays of the year. The butchy lesbian and the chipper gay boy—what a match. No one was going to believe this one. We started to work together and a sexiness appeared in him I'd never seen before. He became harder. I became softer. We started hanging out. He did things for me. That's how he showed he loved me in those early days and also later on. He anticipated my needs, surprised me with his help without me asking. In just a few weeks, he became a home I'd never had. He knew me as I was and loved me as a lesbian. I trusted him.

We began spending all our time together after rehearsals and I stopped going home to my girlfriend. For the first time I felt like myself and so, so safe. He seemed to adore my wildness, found it fascinating, and never in our ten-year relationship did he ask me to change. He always said to me, "You're this free spirit floating around up there, doing your thing, and I'm your mattress when you fall out of the sky. I'm just waiting here to catch you again and again and again." Those words were spoken as if they were the most tender compliment (which they were).

There was no malice ever. He was my very best friend and the first person I really felt I could count on. My parents are really good at love-talking and buying you things, but they don't *do* things for you.

We had to make out in the play and the kiss wasn't the best. That was disappointing, but I didn't care. This time it wasn't really about sex; it was about a person, and I found myself craving his company, his friendship, flirtation, and even the not-so-great kiss during the shows. The critics said we had palpable chemistry onstage. I thought we did, too.

I left my girlfriend, and Jaume and I went to New York together to do the same play off-off-Broadway. It got canceled and we had six weeks together to just hang out. I stopped drinking, and not because he asked me to. Okay, I didn't stop drinking but drank one drink or max two and then we stayed up all night, drinking coffee till dawn, wandering around Manhattan most days, dreaming and talking and writing and not wanting to separate from each other, ever. The number of cigarettes I smoked was more than halved as well—again, not because he asked me to. We started sleeping together and he invited me to come to Spain for a month. I went. I never came back.

He wasn't gay. Neither was I.

I forgot my computer today, so I'm sitting here (in a grotty bar in Sants, a working-class neighborhood in Barcelona where Ava has her gymnastics class) speaking into my phone, reminding myself what I want to write to you about later…

There is this look that's so characteristically Spanish: olive skin, then auburn/blonde hair dye over what is naturally very dark, coarse hair. Depending on the woman, the coloring can vary in tone from light to dark copper. That skin tone and that copper coloring just don't match. Stick to what you were born with: it always looks better, and nature designed you that way for a reason. Once, at Jaume's request, I dyed my hair that copper color, and it didn't work on me, either. I don't have an olive complexion; it's ruddy—even worse.

In general I've been told I'm pretty but normal-pretty. I take that as a little above average. Most days I don't feel pretty and don't notice anyone looking at me as if I were.

I'm not looking. That could be a seduction/an invitation if I did.

Random people, friends, a few lovers have said I'm "sexy," which comes out when I drink and move without any inhibition and manage the dance floor; later, my behavior disgusts me, because it reminds me of Kitty.

I have a recurring dream: I'm a model; photos of me are published in a magazine. The final confirmation of my beauty. I feel a sense of relief.

I'm serious at work, then at night with my friends the other Samantha comes out: the fiery, confident one, the one who doesn't give a shit, the one who makes her own rules and makes people say and do things they wouldn't normally say or do. I seduce men and women alike. I don't want to do anything with them physically; I just want them to want me, to acknowledge that I could do something if I wanted to. It gives me power, and in that moment I feel beautiful. I feel visible when I'm desired sexually. Sometimes when the seduction game has gone a little too far, I tense up and tell them to stop. I go numb and lose interest. I'm not good at one-night stands. I can count on one hand how many I've had. I always hear my mom telling me I'm cheap and slutty and can never go through with the full sexual act.

Come here. Kiss me.
   (They kiss. It gets more passionate. It looks like it's leading to sex.)
   So what do you do? Why don't you give me a little sample of what you do?
   Oh, come on!
   Let's hear a little moaning. Come on, please. Let's hear it.
   Noooo.
   Come on. Pretend. What do you do?
   I can't.
   Yes you can. Come on.
   No I can't. I don't want to.
   (She withdraws, seems vulnerable and self-conscious.)
   It's just a joke. It's just for fun.
   I don't want to be that way with you. I want to be me with you.

That's interesting what you say about Laurie being the strong silent type, because William isn't much of a talker, either. He calls talking "that thing you do with your mouth." He's a sound technician, the first nonactor I've ever been serious about. He isn't drawn to elaborate discussion (on rare occasions he can be, usually with someone who isn't his partner, like that one time with you in London). In that way, he's very stereotypically "English" and "male."

Saw someone in the Metro today: a beautiful black man, sharply dressed—with a little style. I caught his eye and he caught mine. He followed Ava and me into the same wagon and we exchanged glances. I knew there was something there. In the eyes, a mutual recognition. In a nanosecond we knew each other completely and not at all. It made me feel attractive again; I still have it. Would he be bored with me after a brief fling? Would I?

When I was fifteen, Scott screwed everyone at the school behind my back, and when I lost my virginity to him, he gave me chlamydia—my mother's worst nightmare and mine. Well, at least it wasn't AIDS, but boy was I in big shit, and did I get a scare. Now, according to my mom, there was a possibility I'd be sterile. I panicked about that until I had Roc and Ava with Jaume in 2002 and 2004.

My mom still thinks she's getting away with it all. That's the difference between her and me. She actually pretends Kitty doesn't come out to play, or Kitty doesn't drug herself into oblivion because the pain inside hurts so unbearably bad. She's fine and doesn't want you to take away her veil. If she doesn't talk about it, maybe you'll forget it ever happened. And if you try to talk about it, she's a master of confusion/distraction—won't understand you, will make you feel crazy for questioning her behavior. She has magic tactics to somehow not answer any of your direct questions. Simply won't answer any question you ask her. If I persist, she breaks down, cries, and says, "You just hate me, don't you?" Forget it. I know what I do when I escape and I want to figure out why the hell I have to keep escaping again and again, to act wild—in Catalan, *salvatge*. My mom pretends she's not wild, but she is.

Fascinating how, in *The Lover*, Marguerite Duras's mother turns her back to what's really going on. Unable to deal with the situation, she completely encourages her daughter at the same time, in what amounts to an unspoken directive: take advantage of the rich man, but feel terrible about it.

A guy I went to grad school with visited me in Barcelona, and after a couple drinks he announced—in a complimentary, jokey way—"I always thought you were hot and wanted to sleep with you back then." Later that night I told him I'd wanted to sleep with him, too. A lie. I never found him attractive, but I had to make him think the feeling was mutual so he wouldn't feel bad for exposing himself to me. Why?

I'm a weird mix of shyness and fuck-all.

I remember the first time I heard someone actually call me "Trouble." I was shocked. It was almost as though she'd said I was a heroin addict. Friends say if you have a night out with me it's dangerous; we're not going to chat quietly over one glass of wine. Most likely we'll laugh, cry, dance, sing, dress up, and—surely—consume large amounts of alcohol. Forget about doing anything the next day after being out all night with Trouble. I'm incredibly good at getting everyone to follow my manic madness, too. I shower people with attention, make them feel special; I'm a laser beam focused entirely on them, making them happy. Tonight is magic—of course it is! And typically it is. To me it is...

I have a small part (a maid, ha!) in a thriller, which is being shot in France, where I'm emailing from right now. One night, we had a gorgeous meal. Civilized conversation, nothing crazy. Me with the bigwig actors—feeling inadequate, nearly invisible, or wanting to be, keeping myself down, controlled, restricted, while they spoke about their agents in London and Daniel Craig being godfather to one of their sons.

I befriended the couple who run the restaurant and have been responsible for the catering. Every meal has been four courses and divinely delicious. Every day I take pictures to remember what I'm not allowed to eat because I'm starving myself for another shoot next week.

The other night, after everyone left, I stayed on, chatting with Patricia (one of the owners). Next thing you know, my computer was plugged into the stereo system and I had her and her husband dancing their asses off with me to very loud, deep house. Before leaving to go back to my room, I helped her change twenty tables to be set for twelve for breakfast the next day. In the middle of the night, the three of us drunkenly befriended each other on Facebook. She sent me photos of us, showed me her paintings, and spoke of her longing to just be an artist, to leave the restaurant. That night, she'd had a taste of freedom. In the morning, I was sitting there with all the cups and saucers, plates and more plates, the spoons and knives and forks and tablecloths I'd carefully placed three hours before. The following day, she thanked me on Facebook and I couldn't answer.

After nights like that I disappear. A night of boundary-breaking intimacy, and then I go into hiding. The other person takes it as distance, rejection, while I'm horrified I lost sight of the good girl; as the night progresses, I act more and more like a cult leader. I'm humiliated by my loss of control, just like my mother is. The fact that we're not allowed to act *salvatge* makes us binge. No smoking, no drinking during the week: keep it together and perfect and then on the weekend let that caged-up Doberman speed out of the kennel. I can't live up to it all. Am I secretly like Ava, who wants to be left to run wild? To live by her own rules? Yesterday she was angry at the wind. She was punching and kicking and shouting at it. I understood. She feels things and can't keep it in. She has to react. She has to, she says. I do, too.

"I'm getting lonely being with you. The more I'm with you the lonelier I get. That's not a good sign. If I were older and wiser, I'd take a walk. I'd go home, watch *Miami Vice* and feel good about myself. I'd remind myself how good I live without a man. I'd regain my equilibrium. Ever since I met you, my life's been imbalanced, it tips in the love and sex direction. I look at your skin and think I'm gonna have a nervous breakdown if I'm not allowed to touch that man's skin. I meet 10 billion other men a day but I see you, my heart has a little heart attack, I get wet down there"—monologue from Wendy MacLeod's *Apocalyptic Butterflies*, which I did in grad school. Total foreshadowing of my relationship with William.

I'm still attracted to women and probably always will be. I'm lucky I feel comfortable with that, but it turns out I happened to find a man. I don't feel I'm missing out by not being with women, since I tried it out with many partners and explored it for a reasonable amount of time. And to be perfectly honest, the sexual act feels to me more complete with a man.

I definitely don't want to shut down *The Samantha & David Show*. I just think you should ask every question you want to ask, and I should answer every question I want to answer. Good?

I hate feeling invisible. When I asked an ex what he liked about me, he said, "I don't know. I can't really say there's something specific. I just kinda feel your presence [gesturing to the side and slightly behind him] right here." Thanks. Like this antique mirror I had in my apartment, ornately carved cherry wood. When I moved everything out of that apartment and did the last dummy check, there it was. I was so used to seeing it I didn't see it anymore. How could I have not seen it? Is this what always happens in relationships?

I always take mental pictures of my lovers—specific parts of their anatomy, drawing the lines in my mind— to remember them by. I want that look from William we had when we first met. I still have it for him. Why doesn't he have it for me? Almost daily I see him again and again and again and again for the first time. The invisibility sends me into self-loathing.

My mom constantly warns me that Jaume and I need to be really careful in how we handle our divorce. Despite how well Jaume and I are dealing with things, she sends me an article about "parental alienation." I don't know how many times she's made me feel guilty, imagining a sadness in Roc and Ava. I have to console *her—her* grief over *my* divorce. She often tells me how much Ava needs me. I don't see her every day now because of shared custody, so I have supposedly made a selfish decision and the kids are now going to feel abandoned by me.

When I started babysitting at twelve years old, I would look in the mirror at myself and the baby resting her sleeping head on my shoulder. I knew how to comfort her, make her feel safe. I pretended she was mine and took pride in knowing I could look after her. She trusted me. I was there no matter what. If the baby got a diaper rash, I was terrified the parents would think I was sexually abusing her.

I once did a short film in which the mother threw me out of the house for teaching her kid about Jesus; to get into the scene emotionally, I imagined the scenario of an accusation of sexual abuse—one place where I could constructively use my pain and confusion.

Good morning, Miss. I'm the minister's wife. I was wondering if I could come in and give you some information about our church.

No, no, I'm not interested.

I think you'll really like what I have to show you.

No really, I'm not interested.

But you don't know what you're missing. It's really inter-esting. Come on, just give me five minutes.

Well, okay, but only five minutes.

You won't regret it.

I'm doing it again (again). I can't say no. I feel sorry for Milo. I like to be around him and I feel burdened by him. He's leaving in two days and really needs my help. He's newly married and has a newborn baby; he's splitting his time between Barcelona and Ukraine—his ex-wife is in Ukraine. She has the other two daughters to take care of and has cancer. He has no money. He stays out probably once a week, doing coke, drinking gallons of spirits, and "networking." He's 6'4". Just like Jesse. Jesse would like to look like him. Jesse was 6'4" and obese. Milo's not. Milo's kinda hot. He has Carl's aloofness and says completely "inappropriate" things. He's Jesse and Carl combined. Soft and vulnerable, troubled, then hard and selfish and mean and sexy. He makes everyone feel uncomfortable and that weirdly comforts me. It means I can do the same.

On the film set he told me it looks like I work out a lot and have a good body. (I don't know if he actually said that second part; I intuited it.) He then said I didn't have any tits—in other words, *lástima*. His current wife has massive melons. He obviously likes that look better. Carl also liked to point out what was wrong with my body while coming on to me. Milo can pick me up with one hand. I like that. I don't feel fat then.

Another time on the set, after we'd broken for the night, he got me to smoke a joint. I hate smoking pot. It scares me; I've always found it brain-scramblingly numbing. I did it anyway, 'cause I wanted him to like me. He has a way of making me feel a little invisible, even boring, then he hugs me and makes me feel special—without looking at me, though. He's lived through war. I wouldn't know the first thing about how that might change a person. Maybe that's why he's tough and selfish. I don't want to have coffee and listen to his one-man show. I know he wants to meet me so he can use my studio. He's downstairs and I answer the phone after two missed calls from him: "Come down, come on, just come down." I go down, watch him smoke eight cigarettes in twenty minutes, and listen to him talk while he intermittently shoots cookie-monster voices out at his newborn son in the baby buggy next to us. He asks me how I am, then continues on about the disgraces in his life—entertaining stories that have the word *fuckin'* dropped in there every other word. I listen. I feel bad. I feel drained.

A month later, he wants to meet again. I don't have time to record a voice-over job for him, because I have my own deadlines and kids to take care of that day, but I do it, anyway. As he leaves, he asks me when we're going to party again, picking me up and lifting me way above the ground in a very affectionate hug. I hug him back and call him "sweetheart," like I really care about him. I know he's just using me and pretend I don't notice. I still want him to like me. These kinds of people are magnets. They get me every time.

Not sure what I think about the Robert Stoller quote you sent me: "The major traumas and frustrations of early life are reproduced in the fantasies and behaviors that make up adult erotism, but the story now ends happily. This time, we win. In other words, the adult erotic behavior contains the early trauma. The two fit: the details of the adult script tell what happened to the child."

I don't know if I feel that happy ending in my sexual experiences. Somehow, the trauma taints everything one way or another. I completely agree with you about avoiding the "I was abused and never escaped" moan session, but it has formatted me—it's a filter I have—and right now I find it impossible to not see everything linked to it. Would be great to find some revelation that is cycle-breaking.

I feel like I've spent half my life in therapy.

My mother had, and has, a need to know absolutely everything about what I'm thinking, doing, etc., probably stemming from her own mother's distance. Vivian was married to another man before Errol and had a child, my mom, with that other man at nineteen. They divorced shortly after having my mom, who had to be hidden—sort of the bastard child. Vivian sent my mother to live with her parents from age two to five, and when Vivian married Errol, my mother wasn't allowed at the wedding.

She was told her birth father was a bad man and she wasn't allowed to see him. (He'd come back shell-shocked from World War II and Vivian had no patience with his languor, although he wound up being far more successful in business than Errol ever was.) My mother has a vague sense that some sort of sexual abuse may have occurred, or someone may have suggested to her that it happened, but she could never confirm this.

I remember one morning—I must have been around three—cuddling up to my mom, spooning her and lightly patting her bottom, to comfort her, to show affection, as she'd always done to me. It seemed to me an extension of a hug. Two pats in, she almost jumped from the bed.

She says she was made to feel guilty—by her mother—on the two or three occasions when, as a child, she saw her birth father. They were reunited about ten years ago and continued to have a relationship until he died recently.

Just like her mom, at nineteen my mom had a daughter, whom she gave up for adoption. (Vivian and Errol sent my mom to a pregnancy home in Kentucky to hide herself/it.) This half sister of mine, Sallie, found my mother about eight years ago. They have a relationship now, seeing each other when my mom goes to Detroit, and she's come to Seattle to visit. I think they speak about once a month—probably more than my mom and I do. Sallie wants to meet me. Not interested. That probably sounds really cold, but I'm just not.

I think my mother felt that Errol never loved her. In fact, about twenty years ago she discovered that even though Errol adopted her, she wasn't in Errol and Vivian's will; only Sarah and Eleanor were. I believe there was a confrontation and that was changed; I'm not sure.

Starting when I was around nine—to get my mom to stop drinking—I'd imitate her drinking and vomiting episodes from the night before. Tucking me in at night, she'd be drunk, alcohol on her breath, her dead weight next to me. I'd tell her to brush her teeth. Didn't matter. She wasn't there...

After a week of drugging herself to near death in her room last summer when I was visiting, she appeared one morning with smeared lipstick on her mouth, a wild, high look in her eyes, and a crazed smile on her face, saying, "Hi! Good morning, everyone!" She was *fine*, so *happy*, so *joyous*, and was letting me know with that smile that nothing was going on and nothing had been going on over the past five days. I can still hear it in her voice over the phone and don't trust that she's ever really going to come off her pain meds.

I'm jealous of people who have no need or desire to blot things out. (You really never drink more than one glass of wine with dinner? That's so weird, David!) I've taught myself how to not feel unpleasant things. I've suffered from horrible panic attacks since, really, forever. As a young child I didn't know what they were. I just thought I was dying all the time. For years and years I've been trying to reprogram myself to feel things, pleasurable things. I used drinking, and still do, as a way to calm the negative noise and go into a celebratory mood: *Look how lucky I am to be where I am despite it all. Life is great!* (I'm sober right now, by the way.)

January is No Vices month for William and me. No coffee, no cigarettes, no booze. My skin is all broken out, and I look like hell. I feel hyperactively awake, nervy. I feel super-sharp mentally, which I really like, but sometimes it's just too loud in my head. My normal state is like a person on speed. I drink to calm that down. I've been exercising and that just gives me even more energy. I long to feel fucking *tired*. I'm just never relaxed.

So how long have you been in the business?
    About three years.
    Do you enjoy your work?

Definitely.

Do you like it more with men or women?

Oh, men, of course.

Do you prefer vaginal or anal sex?

Vaginal. If I can avoid anal, all the better.

Do you like being peed on?

I don't get into any of that—S&M, domination, anything that deals with pain. That's just really not my thing. And I won't do it.

Have you ever done any of these things we're talking about?

Yes.

What happened?

I just don't get excited by those things. I enjoy sex a lot, just not that way.

Have you always enjoyed sex?

I lost my virginity when I was twelve and I've always really liked sex. It's just something that comes naturally to me.

Are there certain people you like working with?

It's great when you get to work with someone you have a good connection with. I usually get to choose my partners.

The men always seem to have orgasms, but you can never really tell if the woman does. Do you fake your orgasms?

Well, sometimes, you know, for the film. Even though you may not feel excited, it's important that the person watching the film thinks you are, but I've had orgasms. Really. Lots of *times. If you're with someone you like working with, it can happen.*

What would you say is your sexual fantasy?

I've always wanted to have sex with a complete stranger in a bathroom at a gas station.

In a bathroom at a gas station?

Yeah.

Why a gas station?

I don't know.

Trying to explain to my actress friend in LA why I far prefer rehearsal to performance...

Annie Ernaux's writing is so unpretentious and simple and concise. I like how she occasionally reveals herself in this mysterious way, never giving away too much but letting you in enough to want more. That's a huge difference between French and American culture. Living abroad has made me see the American impulse to talk about everything as veering at times toward the grotesque.

Last night I went to the cinema by myself to see *Amour*, which would never have worked had it been done in the States. Hollywood would have made everything over the top and too revealing, pounding it into the ground. Its sole purpose would have been to be a platform for an actress to win an Oscar. They would have used a forty-something actress to portray an eighty-year-old, transforming her face to show she could "play ugly"; then she'd appear at the Oscars as a Botoxed princess.

In '95, after graduating from college, I moved to LA "to break in to the business" and worked a few nights a week in the bar at Marie Callender's. During a staff talent show, after I got attacked in the kitchen by the head chef, I drove out to a dangerous neighborhood to buy cigarettes. Talking to a bum, smoking in the parking lot, I got that Kill Me Now feeling.

I've been haunted by the article about Lindsay Lohan you forwarded to me. Obviously, she and I are very different. Some of her behavior, though, is very familiar—not the spoiled-brat, diva stuff, but fear of being alone (which her director remarked upon), pushing limits, etc.

Women in LA definitely have their own way of dressing. One step above hooker. They really accentuate their asses.

The women and men in the movies I dubbed were usually so cheeseball. My mother "told" me they're gross and wrong. All the women look pretty much bog-standard: fake tits, blow-job lips, and pretty fit, nothing that stands out to me. The guys are hulky and stupid, shallow, just a dick. One particularly sexy couple sticks in my mind, but I enjoyed watching their chemistry more than I wanted to join in. I crave that chemistry with someone I know.

In college I got really angry in my first Women in Theater class. The typical nineteen-year-old revolutionary phase—discovering all the ways in which women are objectified, suddenly feeling all the frat boys around me, dragging their tongues on the ground at any female— and I wanted to kill them. A bunch of throbbing penises everywhere. I dressed in ways that hid my body and I didn't want anyone to look at me. They were to like my brain, not my face or body. That might have been just another excuse for feeling ugly, to hate them before they could tell me I was ugly.

Suffered through a cartoon dubbing session this morning. Not feeling it at all. Not inspired in any of my work right now. I hate living in this passionless state. I'm boring myself. No highs or lows, just gray and dull. Must be this No Vices month. February is almost here, though.

Medea was exotic. She was half-Chinese, kinda punk, and had already lived in France for a year or two, traveled around, posed naked for pictures (which she showed me), and brought back this French photographer, François, as her husband. She was nineteen. He was huge—stocky and tall—and had a shaved head except for one tiny purple ponytail on top. They were so cool. She used to stare at me in this adoringly innocent way, loved my shiny red lips, told me I looked like a '70s model. To this day, I thank her.

One night, she and another boyfriend (François had gone back to France) and I were sitting around on her bed. This boyfriend was looking at the differences between our bodies as if he were about to draw us both, like the beginning of an adult movie. I was a bit on the

Rubensesque side at that time and she was a waif. He liked my curves, liked her boyish body, and touched our legs simultaneously, stroking them. Because we were all "artists" and young, this was okay in that moment.

It wasn't okay a second later when she left to use the bathroom; he took a nosedive into my neck and I shoved him off. I actually had defenses: I had an instinct that kicked in and said no instead of freezing and conceding. The "normal" thing would have been to do what he wanted, to make him feel all the things he wasn't: attractive, desired, sexy. It would be normal to say "yes" because "no" could turn to violence. My half sister Rebecca had trained me how to respond to an "aggressive" male. When she was raped by a guy, she told him how much she loved what he was doing to her, saying how good it felt. She'd practiced that technique over and over with Carl until one day she couldn't handle it anymore, moved out, and got her own place at sixteen. I guess it didn't work out so well, but, anyway, the fight is what they want. It's the no. Apparently, this reverse psychology works like a charm when trying to get a rapist to stop raping you.

One night, Medea came to a party at my house. We sat on my roof outside the kitchen, smoking cigarettes, and she told me, "I got dressed up for you." I was beautiful in those words. Everything she said seemed like it came out of a six-year-old's mouth. You know how you laugh when little kids say something "grown-up"? That's how I felt every time she spoke. She didn't understand why people laughed at her. Nor do six-year-olds. We talked about how neither of us had ever had sex with a woman, giggled, and made out next to the stereo system. We lost our girl virginities together. I didn't once feel like saying no that night. There was no baddy in the room. No threat. No danger. Her pussy wasn't "perfect" (whatever that means), and that imperfection became even more perfect for me. She didn't know it wasn't, or maybe thought it was, or simply didn't care. That was liberating for me. I came and didn't tell her. I loved every minute of it and loved myself and my sex a little more after that.

We saw each other the next Monday or Tuesday, whatever day it was in our Women in Theater class. I felt a twinge of jealousy, thinking someone else could have her and she might turn her adoration away from me, but she was mine.

I'm comfortable when I know I'm doing what makes the other person happy. I like to be directed; I used to get off on that (not in a sexual way) with directors. Maybe it was that if I could do exactly what they imagined, it gave me power. I could see a look in their eyes—a recognition that I'd understood exactly what they were saying; there was a look almost of disbelief that I could get it so quickly, which was a sort of intimacy in itself. They felt understood, and I was helping them externalize/realize their ideas. Perfect intimacy-junkie scenario, really.

I like that I left a dinner party to talk more into my phone...

My half sisters, Rebecca and Louise, were my idols. Louise and I were never very close, but I wanted to be. She was seven years older, had thick, dark brown hair and the same legs I have. I secretly wished she was my twin. She was gorgeous before she got in an accident at seventeen, on her prom night; a drunk driver in a semi smashed into her car. The right side of her face was partially paralyzed. Her mind was never the same, either. She was skittish. After the accident, one of her eyes was smaller and she looked like she was winking at you all the time. She accompanied that twitchy winking with a shrieking laugh, as if it were all on purpose. I talk about her as if she were dead.

About a week after my nauseating Thanksgiving encounter with Carl more than twenty years ago, Louise called me. This was the very last time we spoke, she and I. "Samantha? Sam?" She had this knowing-hushed-panicky thing going on in her voice. "What happened?" She knew what had happened even before I told her. That day on the phone, I romanticized this link, the abuse link—a sixth sense she had for another suffering sibling who'd undergone what she'd gone through for years. She knew how I felt. "I knew it. I knew it. Sam, you don't owe them anything, okay? Just stay away from them."

She told me she no longer talked to either of our brothers. Maybe they were next to her with a gun to her head. Maybe she helped in the planning of it all. My half sisters have always been jealous of me, and a little suffering might do me good. My brothers and sisters all have that David Lynch perverted-clown look. Something definitely off-kilter.

Carl is following my public Facebook posts. I couldn't help it and had a look through his Facebook photos and videos—which was like licking a battery. One video he titled, *Awwww even my mom likes this one.* Two teenagers are outside a house and the guy asks the girl to give him a blow job. She says she can't because they might get caught by her parents. The boy's hand has been on the intercom the whole time and the family has been listening to the conversation. Suddenly his little sister opens the front door and says to the girl, "My dad says will you just get on with it or he says he'll come down and give him the blow job or even I can do it, but please just give him the blow job." What's that "Awwww" about—suggesting it was a "cute" video? That he and his mom had an innocent, nostalgic moment watching this together? How many blow jobs did Carl's mom give him?

On Facebook, there's a picture of Carl (or "Karl," as he now spells it) sitting on a kitchen floor in his underwear, his matted hair standing straight up, a crazed, sick look on his face, as he holds a half watermelon that looks like it's been ripped apart, not sliced. He's been eating it by shoving his entire face in it. It's all over him. Another video is a close-up of one of his eyes. It pans out and we see his whole Buffalo Bill face. He says very eerily, "Hellll-looooo." I consider myself a pretty intuitive, empathetic person and I don't understand what he's doing in any of these videos. It's a code I can't break, yet it's completely familiar. They disturb me and I'm compelled to look at them again and again. Am I seeking pain by watching these videos, trying to relive that darkness because it's the only thing that feels really real?

About ten years ago, Carl told my dad he was married to two women and they all lived together. Rebecca told me their mother openly had sex in the front room with various partners during the day and the kids just came and went as they pleased, observing it all.

One day, when I was five, we dropped off my four half brothers and sisters at their mom's, my dad's ex-wife's house—Karin. Not "Karen." Karin. As we pulled up, she came out into the street in a négligée with nothing under it. I saw her nipples and pubic hair and remember thinking the hair down below was darker than the red hair on her head. My own mother went rigid. Actually, I think she might have started to yell at Karin, who sang a hello to my parents like a prostitute saying how much she'd charge to be fucked up the ass. That was one of the first times I saw sex being used as a slithery weapon. In the same voice, she'd call our house day in, day out: "Hiiiiiiiiiii, Saaaammmaaanthhhhaa, what are you dooooing? Is your daaaddy home, hooonnneeyyy?" This skanky, twisted Cruella de Vil wedged herself into our house, causing endless fights between my parents until one day my dad took her to court and got a restraining order put on her.

At my tenth birthday party, Rebecca, around twenty-one at the time, couldn't help herself and randomly asked all the girls if they knew what a blow job was. I could hear

Karin in her voice as she explained to all of us that it had nothing to do with a blow dryer. She then made sure we really got it by miming the act as if the cock she was sucking were twenty inches long and so wide she could barely get her mouth around it. She laughed a nasty, sexy laugh. All of my friends went silent. My humiliated parents barked at her.

Sometimes when I'm lying in bed, my body turns to stone and I feel like it's such an effort to crack out of the position, to move my arms just the tiniest bit. I have the need to jump, to twitch, to shake my body to keep it from freezing up again. Sometimes it's so intense my body feels as though it's being crushed by two cement walls. Awwww.

There are some kisses where they kiss only with the tongue and others that are the "dive-in" type, meaning heavy breathing, like taking a bite out of something. He pulls off his own clothes really fast and attacks her body with squirrel-like energy—really fast movements. She gets more excited and gives him a blow job, very enthusiastically. This goes on for what seems like ages. She gives him a look, like, "Jesus Christ, how long is this blow job going to last?!" Finally, he goes down on her and she says, "My god, I thought you'd never go down there. I was dying for you." She goes into "ecstasy" and starts doing the Dolly Golden face.

Do most people lose their primal attraction for the other person after six months? Eighteen months? I didn't want to live the rest of my life that way with Jaume, avoiding him (sexually). Extremely weird that he and I were able to do this scene together two months after we split up—

MATTHEW: Lisa, wow. It's been—
LISA: Years.
MATTHEW: Yeah—four years. And you're still—
LISA: Finishing your sentences.
MATTHEW: So it worked out, your marriage?
LISA: Yeah.
MATTHEW: I'm glad for you. Really.
LISA: And you?
MATTHEW: Nothing to report.
LISA: Four years, and there's never been—
MATTHEW: Only you.
LISA: Matthew—
MATTHEW: That's what happens, Lis; there's always one who wakes up first.
LISA: I have to go.

It's a Friday night. Have been chain-smoking cigarettes and drinking wine. Roc is at a sleepover and Ava is in bed.

I'm alone for a mere four hours if I'm lucky. William is out for the night, late, I hope, and I've been calculating how much I drink. One glass an hour. That seems sensible, right? It's been three hours now. I'm keeping a journal of my drinking, per suggestion of my therapist, to see if my drinking is only circumstantial or indeed pathological. On a good, manic day, it's circumstantial; on a down-spiraling day, it's pathological.

I'm wondering if William is going to come home tonight (most definitely drunk and having drunk three times as much as I have), look at the empty wine bottle (some of which he consumed) in the recycling bin, and give me grief tomorrow morning. He's like the controlling dad I never had, which really irritates me. Hence the adolescent rebellion on my part.

I'm a satellite hovering around the house, clicking photos of my three planets, mediating constant screaming matches between Roc and Ava, trying to keep William's temper down, placating him. (I read somewhere, probably through someone's Facebook link to the equivalent of a *Seventeen* magazine article, that one of the things you should do to keep a relationship alive is buy things at the grocery store they really like—it's the little things—so I try to keep his skim milk stocked, buy him peanuts for his hunger mood swings, though not always as he has high cholesterol, have a supply of those little anchovy-marinated pickles. He doesn't notice the flow of milk but gave me a little knowing smile the other day about the pickles. Endearingly tender all of this, isn't it?) And then I'm shushing the kids, "William's working, William's hungry and moody, William can't be distracted…" Eggshells eggshells eggshells—all this tiptoeing around is torturously familiar. William has the back of the house and the kids have their half. My space is the hallway, where I pace back and forth. Over the last few years I've been drinking much more heavily than I ever have in my life. Very, very healthy. Why is William in a mood when I'm buying him his pickles and keeping myself and the kids out of his way? I'm determined to figure out what I can do to alleviate his pain. I'm wired to seek out and love, to my own detriment, the damaged, the wounded, the ones with very little if any empathy. Oh god, I was just about to sneak out for the last cigarette of the night, but Ava's sneezing now. A wander down the hall is imminent. Alone time is over.

The problem with being in a monogamous relationship, especially once you've entered middle age, is that not only will you not be with anyone new but you won't be new with anyone, either. I don't just mean new to the person that you would theoretically be with; I mean new to yourself. Being with a new person can be an exploration of yourself; it makes you new to you. It seems to me one of the difficulties with marriage—and one of the reasons I'm not sure I want to ever get married again, to William or anyone else—is the way couples stop talking to each other the way they once did. Either because you don't want to enter into a certain conversation or because it's too much effort, so you end up being a couple that talks, but not really about anything too close to the bone, and all you get is a kind of distance. It's like being in a long-distance relationship, in which you're forging a separate life (maybe even a bit of a separate identity), but without the physical distance. That's why I think some marriages can make more sense after an infidelity, because that emotional shock acts as a kind of circuit breaker. Loss and fear of loss are put back into the equation. In a sense, the marriage becomes new again because it's suddenly unknowable.

If a wife avoids speaking honestly with her husband about her doubts, desires, etc., is it because she doesn't want him to hear what she has to say, or she doesn't want to hear what he may have to say? And why avoid that conversation? I mean, what else are you avoiding if you're avoiding that conversation? The thing is, marriage—any relationship—is just really complicated, for men and for women, and everyone seems to pay lip service to that reality without actually believing it. Or something.

What do I know? What's your take?

Hello.

Hi.

(Hesitant, sexy, put-on voice) I put these on for you.

(Formal and timid) Take those panties off.

Why don't you take them off?

At age five I was obsessed with seeing other girls' genitals. I still am. Mine are all wrong and damaged. I remember noting the differences in labia, "fat ones" and "skinny ones." Mine were skinny. Fat were better. They were more childlike and innocent.

Around the time my mother taught me how babies were made, I was given a worksheet in my kindergarten class in which we had to number several series of three pictures: an egg, a chick, and a hen; then a seed, a little sprout, and a tree. Etc. Upon completing the worksheet, we were to stand on the carpet. Everyone finished the exercise in thirty seconds—even the dumb kid, John, with the big bald head. They were all high-fiving him and laughing about how it was the easiest exercise ever. I sat there, sweating, and finally just handed in the paper blank. The teacher yelled at me to get back to my table and finish the exercise. All heads turned; mortified, I randomly numbered all of the pictures without knowing any answers and never spoke again in class.

Later that day, I accidentally walked into the bathroom while the dumb kid, John, was pooping on the toilet. He looked at me as if I were an aggressor, as if I'd come in there to check out his willy, which I hadn't. I swear I hadn't. I wanted to die. Throughout my university studies, I never spoke, unless forced to; I was the dumb kid.

I don't feel the same need my mother did to know absolutely everything about what happened every moment the kids were away. Most of the time I ask briefly how their day went and let them tell me, or not. They often tell me they just don't feel like talking about it.

Ava seems overly concerned about appearing sexy, pointing out girls in her class who "are"—at eight—and she won't wear skirts unless they're green or blue. Anything pink or purple she feels draws attention to her. It's like she's already aware of female objectification. Did I somehow pass that fear of being looked at down to her without even knowing it? At the same time, when we were on the plane coming back from the States, she brushed my hair very carefully, tucked one side behind my ear, tilted my head at a specific angle, and then said, "Now, Mommy, stay like that, and let aaaaall the boys *stare* at you." She seemed to take pleasure in thinking the boys would stare at me. Lately, she studies the men on the street studying me and imitates the way they stare me up and down, then asks me if I noticed what they did. She's simultaneously attracted to and repulsed by this female-hunting male. Ava and I went together to a frozen-yogurt place, and after we sat there in silence for a while, I asked her, "What is this feeling you have that dressing in a feminine way somehow makes you sexy?" She said, "I just don't like it... I don't know... Well, I have a secret, but I'll never be able to tell you." Immediately, alarms went off and I thought, *Okay, that's it—here we go—she's been abused; I've been waiting for her to tell me and now I'm going to get her to tell me what happened.* I did what my mother did with me: told her she could talk about anything with me, I'd never judge her or love her any differently, and perhaps I could help her/understand her better if she shared what she felt was such a secret. Maybe she'd actually enjoy sharing her secret (intimacy junkie intimacy junkie). Finally she told me she wanted to be wild: to look dirty and have torn, stained clothes, messy hair (later that evening she identified the exact sublime look in *Pirates of the Caribbean*). She also said she'd like to be an orphan but felt bad about wanting that because she still wants me to be her mommy. She had all these stories about orphan kids in her head and wanted to make a movie with all her friends—not write it, just make it. (Lately, she's been writing stories with related themes). So *wild* was the answer. Not abuse. My projection.

(Remember, David, we agreed we'd redact what I went on to say here about Ava—which pains me, as it completes the female family-cycle puzzle. As her mother, though, I have to protect her. It's not my story to tell; it's hers.)

She speaks openly about how the boys at her school like her and want her to be their girlfriend, and is extremely affectionate. Meanwhile, Roc, when there's a movie on and there's an embrace, or a loving glance between two people (not even a kiss), he hides under the pillow as if someone were being violently murdered. He doesn't want to be kissed or kiss anyone.

It wasn't until very recently that Ava even wanted to have girlfriends. She wanted to play only with boys, impress them, be one of them. She told me she doesn't want to grow breasts, doesn't want her period, and doesn't want to have a baby, because the idea of giving birth is terrifying. She tended to go for all the rough boys in her class. One second, they were friendly; and the next, saying cruel things to her, hitting her, and daily she'd be in tears. Walking to school one morning when she was seven, she asked me, "Mommy, how do you find the person you are going to marry? What happens if you fall in love with someone and they're mean to you all the time?" I told her this time was for practicing, to be able to identify those people who treated you that way so you wouldn't make that mistake when you were older; soon, her radar would be so strong she'd see those hurtful ones immediately and wouldn't even want to be friends with those types of people. That seems to have worked, as she's no longer friends with the bullies and has a group of lovely little girls as friends.

She tells me she wants so badly to be loved by Roc; she loves him so much and he doesn't love her. She's constantly waiting for the opportunity to catch him by surprise and give him a cuddle, because he never wants to cuddle her. She's jealous when he hugs me. This seems to be the pattern she was creating with all the bully boys:

trying desperately to get them to love her, even though they rejected her.

Shrink to a guy I know: "Tell me what images you masturbate to, and I'll tell you who you are."

The look in the eyes when a person comes is that place between life and death. A long, momentary surrender to a soul-trapping ghost—taking the person away, sucking them into a pleasure vacuum, echoing crows cawing. In Spanish they say, Me voy, me voy. "I'm going, I'm going." Which seems more accurate than "I'm coming, I'm coming." No you're not. You're leaving. Leaving together. Being able to make someone go to that place of surrender feels powerful to me. I feel bad for thinking that.

With women, I was viewed mainly as a femme. In my one serious lesbian relationship—with Jessica (and I'm going to have to pull a veil over that as well; lo siento…)—there were no roles per se; each of us was equally dominant and submissive. Initially, I've been quite aggressive in all of my sexual relationships with men and women. I always start off dominating, taking control; then, if the relationship continues, that role disappears and I become the submissive. My sense of humor goes, too. I'm unable to be a clown around people I'm in love with—don't want to turn them off—but a huge part of me is a clown, which I wish I had shown more of to you in our exchanges.

The creator of the TV-series-in-the-making (for which I did that teaser) is actually meeting with Lionsgate, which means they'll surely recast it. I'll send you the link so you can check out how comfortable I was (wasn't) in the "making of" video about being the sex kitten. The edit is classic. They cut me off just as I clown-face apologize for being cast as what should be sexy.

Lindsay Lohan's circular self-destruction: She really needs to be working—that's when she feels the best—but she has to fuck it up by staying out till 5 a.m. with Lady Gaga and then have her doctor come by and say she has an ear infection and will be out for the day. I don't have her resources, I can't cover up the way she does (although it's completely transparent), but I've also gone into work in abominable states the next morning, out of pride: *You did it; you deal with it.*

Being a mother has definitely reined me in. (This last line is Good Samantha, hoping you don't think I'm LL.) I'm sure if I had her money, I'd do everything she does.

I suddenly see myself as a ridiculous, attention-seeking, unstable alcoholic. Surely everyone can label me. They do: "Trouble." Would I prefer "Head-together Sam"? *She's controlled. She's moderate. She's even-keeled. She's nice, but not someone you'd call to have a good time.* I don't know.

I remember being about eight or so—in the car on the way to church—and having a screaming meltdown. I was really angry about something (probably my mother's embarrassing, drunken behavior the night before) and sobbing. My dad screeched the car to a halt and shouted, "That's enough! You're going to stop crying, goddamnit! And when we get out of the car, you're going to put a smile on your face!" Moments later, I got out of the car and posed outside the church for a family photo with a smile on my face, as though nothing had happened. We were perfect and happy.

I loved the first part of Anne Enright's *The Forgotten Waltz*; I literally laughed out loud and cried at the same time. She hits a nerve for me when she talks about sex, adultery, alcohol, guilt. She writes what I think but never say (publicly).

Why am I hiding all the time?

Ani DiFranco:

> *We don't say everything that we could*
> *So that we can say later*
> *Oh, you misunderstood*
> *...*
> *We lose sight of everything*
> *When we have to keep checking our backs*
> *I think we should all just smile*
> *Come clean*
> *And relax*

I work best when there's no tiptoeing around, so I appreciate that you haven't held back. It focuses me and strips away everything superfluous. Shut up and get to the fucking point.

When I was twelve, I was told I was going to have to wear a back brace. (I know you've had your own back issues.) I can remember the doctor's visit—a numbed-out, bass-less heartbeat in my ears, like a speaker with the volume turned all the way up but no music coming out, just that raspily whispered *ehhhhhh* sound. If someone were to press PLAY, the sound would blow everyone out of their seats. I heard the doctor give me the diagnosis, the fuzzy-speaker noise over his gibberish keeping me a safe distance away from what he was saying.

I wore my brace religiously; it never occurred to me to do any different. I'd been sentenced. I accepted it and adapted. Making me wear a brace was just another thing someone else decided to do to my body. Something else to paralyze me.

I have a need to scream almost all the time.

My body and thoughts curl into one another again and again and again. A constant figure eight; there's no end to the circularity. My spine's trying to hug itself. It's a snake trapped mid-slither, squirming its way out of the pain.

Will I ever look at anything as not sick? It's fucking exhausting. I'm fucking exhausted.

In graduate school we were asked to do a life-or-death improv in which the end result would be you naked onstage. People chose situations like gas chambers in concentration camps, or there's a fire in your house and you suddenly have the brilliant idea to take all your clothes off, tie the pieces together to make a rope, and escape out the window, etc., etc. The exercise wasn't optional. Our acting professor was quite intimidating, and you just did what he said. This was part of being an actor—being able to be naked onstage—and we better be prepared for that. Of course I, particularly, was terrified.

We all started saying we just weren't comfortable doing this; the exercise should definitely be optional; it was a little weird and maybe even a little creepy, etc., etc. And then it went sensationalist Puritanical American. Now it was a *violation*. Everything is in America: it's dangerous, it's scary; people kidnap you, they rape you. There's always an underlying agenda, and even if there isn't, you should always be wary. This is how our thinking evolved about this exercise we'd been asked to do. Next thing you know, the sexual-harassment committee on campus was contacted (actually, I think my socially minded boyfriend was the one who made the call), and the committee asked for a meeting with all the students and faculty of the grad program. Our acting professors, who'd been put in an incredibly uncomfortable position, called off the assignment, probably fearing they'd lose their jobs. Phew. No one was going to do it. I was saved. But then suddenly everyone felt awkward. We remembered we were in drama school, not business school. After all, standard social conventions don't apply in The Theater. Were we just scared and using this committee to get out of it?

Now that it wasn't mandatory, the group suddenly craved the challenge and decided to organize a special class outside of class, and whoever wanted to participate in the exercise could. My socially minded boyfriend who made the call to the committee was the first one to say he was in. What the fuck? I was trapped again. I was going to have to do it. I had to do it—not as an acting exercise but because I couldn't bear the thought of him being naked in front of everyone and me not being there. I couldn't handle the thought of him seeing the other girls naked. And I didn't want to miss out on the taboo experience as a viewer. He wasn't allowed to have an intimate experience without me. We got in a huge fight about it. I pretended I wanted to do the exercise when, deep down, I felt sick about having to expose my body to the other classmates—well, to the men. My private parts were incredibly private; if they saw them, my classmates would know what had happened to me.

In *Code 46*, a girl has a virus that makes her physically repulsed by the man she loves. She asks him to make love to her when all the while her body is thrashing around, violently rejecting his. For me, each piece of clothing I removed during that exercise was an act of violation. My body, my guts were screaming *no*, but the virus inside me "wanted" to do it.

We all went out for a drink afterward to talk about it. I was in a sort of shock state. Everyone thought it had been a revolutionary, cathartic experience, whereas I'd just publicly humiliated myself. I wished the life-or-death improv would have killed me with all my clothes on.

The whole time America has believed it's under "constant threat of attack" for its choice to be "free," I haven't lived there.

I went to a photo shoot with a friend, Elena, who was one of the models, and there were a couple guys who were assisting the photographer. I'd met both of them in a bar with Elena a few weeks before the shoot and they seemed accessible and warm, intelligent; we had some candid but "normal" conversations. She already knew them, so conversation went to a more intimate level, as she tends to talk to people that way as well.

The photographer started shooting her, and one of the guys sat next to me on one of the couches and started making really derogatory remarks, saying we were all going to do a *Playboy* photo shoot together. There was a gang-rape tone to the way these two guys were getting excited and talking about us: "Hey, ooh yeah, this is gonna be a fun shoot today" sort of remarks, that all-knowing "You like that, don't you?" kind of laugh.

Eli and I had come from a Spanish lunch, where each of us had had a couple glasses of wine. One of the guys started telling me he could smell alcohol on my breath and somehow found himself right behind me, rubbing my shoulders as if to prep me for his idea of how this photo shoot should go. I felt paralyzed; he made me feel like a prostitute who'd just shown up, and he was going to have his way with me. First he would put me down, to make me feel weak, vulnerable. I tried to go with the flow, as I do in these situations. If you react strongly, he might get violent, so better pretend a shoulder massage is totally normal when it's not. I unparalyzed myself after a couple minutes of his shoulder-rubbing. His body was way too close to mine, and I moved across to the other side of the room, shaking, and sat silently behind the photographer. I left feeling like I'd been violated.

Eli left horrified as well, but whenever we ran into him in the neighborhood, she didn't seem to give it much importance and would just strike up a conversation with him, as though nothing had happened. Did I feel a violation that wasn't there? Did his words and actions penetrate me and not her? I was incapable of looking at him and hated him. A rage seared up inside me for months for not having responded to him—for not having told him to get off me.

Last week I went to a barbecue and there he was, the masseur. I immediately felt the space close in on me. I quietly pointed him out to William, who said, "Okay, relax, I was just talking to him and he seemed like a completely normal guy. You don't have to talk to him, and you don't have to be scared, either. I'm here. Also, people can change. This is your past talking here, sensing danger, the abuser, when there isn't one."

Rather than ignoring him, after an hour or so, I went up and introduced myself again to him. He pretended he didn't know who I was. I didn't need to make things right with him. He should have been the one to do that. I needed to control the situation and make him human again, not a threat. Rather than holding my ground, I went to him.

Just like I wanted to tell my brother everything was okay. To protect the abuser. That. Is. So. Fucked. Up.

I can feel when I'm weak, and the loonies on the street sense it. I get approached, they talk to me, try to engage and get in there, to that soft, vulnerable place, fuck around with it, and I'm always shocked, even though I know it's going to happen before it does. There is this sixth sense, this magnet to darkness, and I find myself frozen, terrified for my life, again and again and again. To be honest, this doesn't happen so often anymore, but for most of my adult life, I've felt like burned on my forehead was a sign: INVADE HER—IT'S YOUR RIGHT.

Sound of a gunshot... Forcing a smile, as "you are your thoughts and expressions"... Still here, though... Feeling much better now after starting in a flat place and pushing through... Don't want to fizzle out toward the end...

I saw Milo again today. For the last few months I haven't picked up the phone when he calls, so he sent me an SMS: a smiley-face-and-tongue-hanging-out-of-the-mouth invite for a "girls' night out!" I tried something new and responded unapologetically with "I'm on kid lockdown mode—can't." "Can't you sell them?" he asked, to which I didn't reply. So, you know, in accordance with my new tactics, I actually flagged him down today as he rode his bike down the street, this guy, this flash, dashing monster on wheels. Guilty, addicted, like a moth to flame—there must be another expression. I emphatically suggested lunch next week. Not dinner. I'm getting better. Right?

It's been building for a while now and yesterday William and I directly discussed it: we're in the process of deciding whether we can be together. I'm just trying to get through each day with work and kids.

Heading to the cinema now to clear my head and/or fill it with things that have nothing to do with all this…

Watching actors in a film, I watch their backs/shoulders when they're listening to the other actor who has the close-up. I watch to see if I can see them breathing, how quickly or slowly, or the pulse in their neck—makes them real. On airplanes or buses or Metros, same thing: I'm constantly checking to see if I can see someone's pulse and the rise and fall of their chest. I don't know why. Maybe to see if they're truly alive. It's an intimacy thing. It's something you hear and see only with your lovers. The heartbeat, the sound of the breath. I can sense a vulnerability if I can see the heartbeat in the neck, see what's really going on in there. I've always felt that the whole world is playing a joke on me, that I'm the only human/nonhuman. Perhaps I'm looking for clues in their vital signs.

When I was six on the playground, I looked down at the shadow my hand was making on the pebbled concrete and had a sudden, overwhelming feeling of not understanding how I got into this body. It was so constricting. I had the feeling that my energy was limitless and was now in a cage. Is my soul trying to connect to something formidably beautiful and larger and feeling frustrated by this physical construct of a human body? Maybe what feels almost spiritual is actually just the manic side of me. Maybe I'm *tocada* ("ill"). In the eyes during sex, I see/feel that same expansive energy I felt at six on the playground. It grows during orgasm and almost leaves the body—the waves of pleasure from head to toe, limitless, infinite. Right now I'm apart from William, but I can sense him, almost be him for a moment, feel him, feel his nose, his mouth as though they were mine. I am him.

We're all star matter, right?

Maybe I should write Hallmark cards.

In grad school we were taught to always make your performance about the other person in the scene with you. Your actions were there only to get something from someone else. It's not about tone or emotion or read or facial expression or posture but desire to make someone else feel something in order to get what you want. In theory, through that approach, something deeper and more honest would always be achieved in the interpretation. You were to forget about yourself. When you forgot about yourself and were focused only on the other person, some very honest things could happen.

I say this so often: "I hear you"...

In an OCD sort of way, I still find myself staring at crowds of people—in a stadium, on a crowded bus, on a pedestrian-jammed street, all rubbing/chafing up against one another—and I think, *They're all here because two people had sex.* All these people. Then I imagine the parents of one person and the parents of another, and then another, all of them passing through their mother's vagina, the most forbidden place on a woman's body. And we're not allowed to talk about that, or look at that, and most definitely not touch that. Especially your mother's, even though we did when we were born. Well, that's how I was raised: to feel shameful about something that, in reality, there is no getting around, or we all simply wouldn't be here. Sex is everything.

My mom sees me as her selfish mother: I'm abandoning my kids, doing what I want to do with my life, and not thinking about how that will affect them, but I'm not sending them mixed messages by keeping them in an abusive household. I need to make her feel okay about how she was (or wasn't) during the abuse and afterward. Which makes me angry. I'm not a victim. I don't feel anything and I'm above it all.

The last few months have been a very rough time in my life, to say the least. Talking about it to you has been nothing but positive. I think maybe it's helped me come out of the cave, at least a little. I'm real. I'm not sick. I'm going to survive. I don't want to be binned. I want to be salvageable.

What I like about doing Shakespeare is he gets how confused everyone is. Definitely not *"Tout comprendre c'est tout pardonner,"* which I think is total bullshit. I'll never forgive Jesse or Carl, nor should I. But before them came Karin. Before my mother came her mother. And before Ava comes me. Line I came across on a bathroom stall in grad school: "Man hands on misery to man. / It deepens like a coastal shelf." Men and their fucking selves. Shelves.

At a casting—a long corridor with benches lining one wall—I sign in at the desk at the end, passing all the models who are here because they've been preselected for having a natural, easy smile and perfect teeth. As have I. They're all sizing me up. I pretend I don't notice, even though I'm painfully self-conscious. I feel inadequate and think they made a mistake calling me in here. I sit down and the guy to my left is the same guy I saw yesterday on the Metro shouting out in accented Spanish an apology for bothering us: he's unemployed and selling his paintings and incense. We're living through an economic crisis and he's a father trying to make ends meet.

He looks like Cameron, my old boyfriend from college—blonde, pale, and thin, but not quite as hot. Nonetheless, he's not your average beggar. I study him intensely. He's suddenly a real person to me, which is horrifying. We could have slept together back then and now look at him. When I watch him audition, I learn he's Belgian. He's supposed to take a bite of this Hershey's chocolate bar and love it. He can't quite muster up anything other than indifference, maybe even dislike. He seems dead. I can't help thinking how much happier he was in the Metro, talking about real stuff. We'll do anything for a stupid chocolate commercial that pays seven thousand euros. All of us.

Remember that film I did this summer? The producer asked if me if I'd like to work with him on a horror movie he's developing. I've never done one. There will be tons of screaming, terrified looks, and I even get possessed at the end. Should be quite hilarious. Going to have to keep myself from being an audience member while acting. It makes me laugh just thinking about it.

David Shields is the author of twenty books, including *Reality Hunger* (named one of the best books of 2010 by more than thirty publications); *The Thing About Life Is That One Day You'll Be Dead* (a *New York Times* bestseller); *Black Planet* (a finalist for the National Book Critics Circle Award); and, forthcoming over the next year, *War Is Beautiful* (powerHouse Books) and *Other People* (Knopf). *I Think You're Totally Wrong: A Quarrel*, co-written by Caleb Powell and published by Knopf in January 2015, has been adapted by James Franco into a film that premiered in May 2015 at Vancouver's DOXA documentary film festival. Shields's work has been translated into twenty languages.

Samantha Matthews is an American actress who lives in Barcelona with her partner and two children.